SELECT

SELECTED POEMS

Margaret Hill

Selected Poems
Margaret Hill

Published by Aspect Design 2016
Malvern, Worcestershire, United Kingdom.

Designed, printed and bound by Aspect Design
89 Newtown Road, Malvern, Worcs. WR14 1PD
United Kingdom
Tel: 01684 561567
E-mail: allan@aspect-design.net
Website: www.aspect-design.net

All Rights Reserved.

Copyright © 2016 Margaret Hill

Margaret Hill has asserted her moral right
to be identified as the author of this work.

The right of Margaret Hill to be identified as the author
of this work has been asserted in accordance with
Section 77 of the Copyright, Designs and Patents Act 1988.

This book is sold subject to the condition that it shall not, by way of trade
or otherwise, be lent, resold, hired out or otherwise circulated without the
publisher's prior consent in any form of binding or cover other than that in
which it is published and without a similar condition including this condition
being imposed on the subsequent purchaser.

A copy of this book has been deposited with the British Library Board

Cover Design Copyright © 2016 Aspect Design
Cover image shows *Summer Seas at Newquay* by
Julius Olsson, RA, (1866–1924) from a private collection.

ISBN 978-1-908832-77-1

CONTENTS

Wartime Children 7
The Outpost 8
War in Galilee 9
Normandy Beaches 10
Those Voices 11
Channel Crossing 12
Ballad of the Laidly Worm 13
The Legend 14
Troy 15
Sutton Hoo Treasure 17
The Mermaid 18
Swimmers' Country 19
Trees 20
On the M25 21
The Bell 22
The Woman's Country 23
The Lamp 24
Miserere 25
A Sense of Country 26
The Well 27
The Abbey 28
Fire Mountains, Lanzarote 29
Turin Museum 30
The Compassionate Stream 31
Sognefiord 33
Winter Solstice 34
Remembrance 35

Fantasy at Chichester 36
The Bonfire 37
Parasols 38
Apples 39
Coast 40
Hands 41
My Arm Teedie 42
Moonset 43
Nouveau Venu 44
Nouveau Venu 45
Ces Chères Mains 46
Those Dear Hands 47
Cantique des Colonnes 48
Song of the Columns 51
Acknowledgements 53

Wartime Children

We came at last out of the smoke,
glad to find the place still standing,
streams sang again down the valleys; [we're singing]
sunlight dappled the forest leaves.

We came out without speaking,
as we had always been taught.
Speech was dangerous in silence,
useless under enemy guns.

We discovered old cottages,
to be restored as remembered.
Roads must wind as they always had;
custom scowled again from her cave.
We obeyed, as before: these things
must be important in some way.

Now over the horizon swarm
the dispossessing young, ready
to tear us bloodily apart.
We turn to our old commanders
for their right hands beside us now,
and surprise folded arms, a small smile,
~~as if, finally, satisfied.~~
Our old loyalty counts for nothing.

The Outpost

It seemed at first a simple wayside shrine,
where country people bring their hopes and flowers;
travellers' reminder of another world,
just like standing stones.

High on a ridge of red, soft clay it stood,
a niche without a wall, and behind it
sunlit waterfalls threw white horsetails
calmly into air.

Up darkening slopes, where deeper shadows moved,
came flowing up a ceaseless stream of ants:
like a black tongue they licked at the shrine to
undermine, destroy the last fragile wall.
But at their touch the red clay liquefied,
melted down in heavy waves to drown the
clicking insect army.

A deadly ribbon, an engulfing stone,
a valley asleep under an empty sky:
nor any sound of rescue on the air.

War in Galilee

They could not know,
those silver tongues in country rectories,
where white doorways frame a cool interior,
white windows fold a green tranquillity,
they could not know
there would be guns, one day, in Galilee.

Galilee guns
will shatter the hills, bite out new skylines,
loosing red soil to stain the once clear lake.
Staunch at ravine and river bend,
small shrubs have kept vigil,
renewing their seed as centuries snowed,
that He might find, unchanged, His once small world.

Carpenters know
the auger's last turn,
the wood feels each one
as a death in itself.

Normandy Beaches

Young breaking waves, wash free these shores,
wipe clean of hurt these long hot sands,
smooth our footprints stitching ripples,
and let the marram take the dunes.

Behind the leafless apple trees
slide weary ghosts in uniform.
Bees' hum mimics the bullet's flight,
branches of trees crack like a gun.
Father and son face each other
across the years, and the battlefields,
both knowing of the other's death.
Icons from past generations
laid down in us, their inheritors.

The wind mourns soft in the cedars:
Light pours from all curves of the sky,
on the rows of crosses marching
obediently to the cliff edge.

Walk with me on the sands;
share the breakers' endless requiem.

Those Voices

This is the day, this is the day
whispered the voices:
when cool breezes will fan the veldt,
the golden lion pace his kopje
with royal, loving paws.

When sun will flood through the fanlight
revealing a hall
swept and orderly, wakening
sleepers to that summer morning
only childhood knows.

When the thread to the labyrinth
will become thick rope,
the central chamber noonday lit,
bowed horns responsive to the palm.

                    But the voices lied.

Channel Crossing

No beauty like the falling wave;
no words to paint the white lace flower
flung back from bows,
and flung again.

No order like the arrowed wake,
binding the boiling sea astern,
turbulent coils,
in taut patterns.

Beauty poised on a bubble of foam,
order laid on dissolving sea:
like winds, like flowers,
call up our tears.

Ballad of the Laidly Worm

The haar hung heavy upon the sea,
The great worm roared in the harbour lee,
Christ hae maircy on such as we!

The haar rolled in upon the toun,
A shield and cover the serpent found
to slide his throat along the ground,
D'ye see it, man, d'ye see it?

Thick white it swirled in every wynd,
the black snake's shadow close behind,
hard to flee and death to find:

The shadow laid its deadly brood
in every street its poison spewed,
hatching its evil as it moved;
D'ye see it, man, d'ye see it?

Till every separate close and stair
showed a separate serpent there,
writhing in glee as it claimed its lair:

The flat headed snakes their vigil kept,
all that night while burghers slept,
in their dreams small children wept;
who woke in terror to find, like a dart,
a little black snake in their darkened heart:
D'ye see it, O man, d'ye see it now?

The Legend

Coming into harbour in the old town,
its green headland rising behind, windblown,
see where, layered in rock, a girl still sleeps.
Though days of may with their torch processions
have come and gone uncounted, still she fails
to lift her head in spring.
                          And yet, they say,
the sea will one day rise to lip the turf
and through that moving deep will stride a king.
Sea flowing from his shoulders like a cloak,
he'll call her down. This time, she'll rise, step down,
brush through breaking waves: take his hand.

Glimpsed on the horizon in scudding rain
when sky and sea whisk up their cloud cocoons,
they'll walk the ocean's restless boundaries:
her steps will encourage the plodding tides,
his prints heal the seabed cracks: such powers
reconcile outward laws and inner fires.

Troy

Yellowing leaves frame the far Dardanelles,
closing the circle on their jostling tides.
Over Tenedos the slanting sun throws
lengthening shadows on once Greek beaches;
Priam's agony is rain on the wind:
the death of Hector, morning's memory.

The setting sun draws down, night following,
more than these half-seen ghosts, who roar and fight
soundlessly on the lonely, broken walls.
It milks the sky of light, earth of colour,
and even memory's glittering stream
sweeps down at last beneath the western bar:
leaving only stars to stare at the grasses
hissing over the tumbled stones of Troy.

agamemnon

Agamemnon's laughter echoed round the tomb.
'They'll always get it wrong now, Clytie mine.
Myth and symbol, structure and archetype,
they'll one day find in our strange story.
They'll never know the simple lust for war,
wind, rain on the cheeks, sight of enemy towers,
heart and strength in line behind the blade.
Indeed, my daughter died—bright sacrifice,
who lit glorious roads to all our dying.
You gave me yours: I killed her as I must:
when I strode home, you killed me, as was just.
Now rolling plains and silver seas beckon
eternally. Your laugh chimes sweet with mine.

aeneas

After the last clinch, the roll of credits,
the honeymoon journey to the Eden
reserved for successful lovers, second son
steps forward to take their chores, chair meetings,
write letters, keep us in our steady furrows.

So Aeneas, quiet soul, after all those
magnificent entrances and exits
of Hector, and despairing Hekabe,
Achilles and proud, crumbling Priam,
simply saved his son, father, household gods,
and steered his people through waters and winds:
on whom no bright glory rests, only an
aura of a lost and remembered Dido.

Sutton Hoo Treasure

You, who swore at rowers a thousand years ago
—thumbs stuck in that belt bright with enamel—
why did you lift your head for western isles?
sniff satisfied grunt at easterly winds?
Cold on your back the white spray whipped,
dealing death-knowledge as the bows surged
over the greening seas. 'Faster,' you bawled,
to mask a leader-lonely fear.

Your brother found his anchorage in seas
mercifully warm to a dying body,
where today the waves jostle and argue still.
You, your haven in soft embracing earth,
lit by westering sun, with honour
and grave goods high. Which we now see.
Your memory lives while we have eyes;
your answer echoes our own longings.

The Mermaid

Stiff leggéd they walk on the earth,
and I, who was once half a fish,
for love slit up my glittering tail,
walked upright on my separate fins,
anguished, aching, in sand-raw air.

Water is there in abundance,
leaping, lying, running past houses,
but they warn their children away
from the tumbling, abandoned rain:
cowering in dried out houses
they hear the deepening note of streams,
the hillsides breathing in relief.

I knew the death they fear: I know
so much the sooner will they feel
the drowning bliss of engulfing seas.

Swimmers' Country

Let your fingers
slide among our moving waters;
let air bubbles
hiss past your cheeks, shouting your name.

Let your tipped hands
gently press apart resistance,
and touch the nose
of a cold, oncoming current.

Light here shafts down
blurred and golden; sinewy shapes
swirl and vanish,
as soft weeds close about your wrists.

Sun and wind rule
the world above, where rock and cliff
incessantly
splinter the seas to flying diamonds.

Water surface
divides these elements, for life
or death. We move
at risk in our other country.

Trees

Against a dark grey sky
towering trees twist and hiss
in a high wind roaring
terror from the west,
as though their hate
could no longer lie
in dark roots, but
must burst upon the air
and wisp to nothing.

And yet they say,
trees cannot hate,
winds do not roar,
they only arise
as pressure requires.

Indeed I know
it is only the wind
that lifts the leaves
which make their sound
in waiting ears.

A sinuous dance in the deepening twilight,
agony of mind and supplication frenzied,
sibilants of malice and slow sap welling,
roots held down by a ram-packed earth,
held fast in hell while the riders pass.

On the M25

Herons' pool and swans' pool open
and close a daily motorway journey.

First a grey circle, ruffled pewter
in the uneasy wind of sunrise.
Gravel banks snarl at the edging reeds,
and herons' wings beat a deeper grey,
heavily, low over the water.

Sunlight fingers the swans' pool,
white birds glide soberly through
sparkling water; round and green,
an island draws up tranquillity.

In between, the dust and metal,
rush of wind, leaves flirting with tyres,
two great snakes which pass in the dark,
headlight and tail their red and white eyes:
death steps delicately from gap to gap,
and, with the sun, surveys his kingdom.

The Bell

Each life dawns
like the chime of a bell, whose note
rings out over the valleys,
to paint its own unique portrait.

The lumbering sun
floods with colour the pencilled hills,
lights the hidden song of water
to a glittering, beckoning stream.

The grave sky
holds in silence the passing hours
till twilight tolls; whose sombre pall
slowly pales to transparency.

Each day folds
its one life under the sunset,
and night takes up the unhurried pace
of time, silent ringer of change.

The Woman's Country

Even you
who know there is such a country,
see only the downs or the high poplars
from a distance.

But we know
where the tiny ripple tugs at pebbles,
the damp of the meadow grass rises
through our fingers.

Overhead
swallows dive for evening insects
dancing challenge to the setting sun
true to nature.

When we speak,
your planes fly low above us, drowning
our words, destroying all hearing.
How will you learn?

We fall silent,
go back to our valleys and woods,
and kneel among them, arms outstretched,
to hold you back.

The Lamp

Black squares of a wide, uncurtained window
frame a lamp, shining out across a lake:
beacon, of course, for sailors lost at night,
running before the wind and driving rain.
But at the edge of sight the flame summons
slithering brown shapes of the drowned, who lift
their sodden heads from dead trees and flotsam
and writhe wearily towards the light.
But for the lamp, the curtains would swing close
against the dark and peering squares,
the lost would drown: the drowned would rest.

Miserere

They always come back in the autumn, ghosts.
Like us, they have a remembrance season.
They watch us, and, unseen, they crowd the air.
They hold out hands, as if hungry for warmth,
to the crimson and bronze of heaped, dead leaves.
The wind pounces, flings them high, spinning: lost,
till falling leaves summon them back next year.

But when I die I'll walk the hills I knew,
Cheviot and Wrekin, and dark Lochnagar.
These are the hills the wind picks clean,
its only interruptors stone and grass
long braced against its heavy sighing;
where the plover's call rises in descant
to the old windsong of all high places.

A Sense of Country

Strange it is,
that it's this ceiling I'm dying under,
not one where I learnt the geography
of my life.

Lying here,
we all draw rivers, ships, islands, faces,
projecting an inner country from our
white oblongs.

Just as strange
the journey here: such alien landscapes,
the hills awry, the rivers dark, sluggish,
the wrong road.

Somewhere else
lay my path, where the contours unfolding
in my mind hailed landmarks, recognised peaks
as old friends.

This ceiling
holds the last match of map to country:
when it dissolves, will it show a void, or
the right world?

The Well

This is the last place we come to,
where all worlds have come to their end;
cast off like loosed mooring ropes,
at the beginning of a journey.
Here the light allows no shadows,
bleak as dressed stone about a well.
Here, air carries no messages,
like deep well water, still and cold,
Held apart, like stone lining a well,
Time no longer flows; merely waits,
for our plunge into dark water.

The Abbey

Keep in mind that stone can only be stone.

Where soaring pillars lift a holy roof,
its arches frame a stained glass parable:
Stone seems obedient.

Where elephant columns trample the earth,
brush apart the faithful, their candles and prayers,
stone seems contemptuous.

Stone remembers the sky, once its own roof,
its sibling rocks, still hurtling round the sun;
now just firefly stars: its young outcrops rising
through the hillside.

Remember, stone is only, ever, stone.

Fire Mountains, Lanzarote

The sound of old pain
rises from these gaping mouths;
huge black O's where scarlet lava
spewed, its very lines and mass
held cold in desolation.
Ribbon tarmac noses past such terrors,
to the only hilltop sanctuary,
where, six feet down,
the fires still rage.

Turin Museum

'The ghosts come out at night, of course,
mill round the showcase, there, in front,
where they punch each other's shoulders,
in a huge, silent laughter at their
brave poses, struck in sepia photos.
All good friends now, feuds forgotten,
they link arms, stroll past labelled lives,
leaving in the air a spice, a memory
of the blazing Risorgimiento . . .
Visitors? Oh, they shuffle around,
droop over the exhibits: they haunt
these rooms from a sense of duty;
no joy, no fury; just half dead:
bring back the Garibaldi years!'

The Compassionate Stream

Fountain of laughter, clearer than glass,
whose winking bubbles flowingly explore
sweet new-made curls of tiny water weed,
baby dews on either bank rise up amazed
to see grace itself so merrily sliding by.

   Little ripples singing over brown stones
lip and tug at soil grains to leave their home,
swirling them round, out to the sunshine,
away from the dappled, secret stream
to the dancing lights of the little river.

Out from the rock exultantly flies
a high, white jet: it dives down to a pool,
leaps up again, to chuckle down the gorge;
spreading at last through pasture meadows
lying smooth between bordering poplars.

   Heavy and slow, the river twists through
reed-edged, narrowing banks; hears a promise
in the roar of breakers; whose mist floats up
to form new clouds, now massing eagerly
for their joyous race to the horizon.

High they come, the cloud leviathans,
heaven's acrobats, rollicking porpoises,
irrepressible whales surfing the wind.
Their shadows move over the mountain flanks,
triggering huge rhythms under the ground,
stirring the peaks to pierce the clouds to rain
scattered bright pools, who wink back at the sky,
in a enormous joke with their fathers.

In slow drops, by subterranean ways,
streams ease themselves down through filtering rock,
building up power, to rise again in a . . .

*fountain of laughter, clearer than glass,
whose winking bubbles flowingly explore
sweet new-made curls of tiny water weed . . .*

Sognefiord

Clouds are veiling the midnight sun,
air lies heavy on the water;
ripples hardly break the surface.
And all around rise up huge mountains,
who saw the glaciers pack their ice
from snow falling soft over time;
who saw them melt, grinding the rocks
to valley slopes and unfathomed fjords.
Scarves of mist nose along the hills,
over the pastures and alps of hay.
While the high mists caress the peaks:
the courtship of cloud and mountain.

Winter Solstice

Coming up to the solstice,
clouds gather at the horizon
smooth and slim like little fishes,
their past turbulence laid aside.
Echoing this winter vigil
pines cluster at the field edges,
where mist folds round them like a cloak.
Our turning world comes to a pause,
as between one breath and the next.
By that stillness, by that silence,
the waiting landscape salutes
the advent of majesty.

Remembrance . . .

It can no longer move us
when you show us all these deaths;
Burnt bodies, or butchered limbs,
shells exploding, mixing earth,
trees, sky, in one monstrous cloud.
We have seen it all before,
when we first endured such sights.
They were our fathers, brothers,
our sons, whose moment of death
is shown again and again.
This frenzy of remembrance
kills even our gentle ghosts.
Let our men lie quiet now,
as though they had never been.

Fantasy at Chichester

All eyes to the lighted stage,
where plays are seen in the round:
all eyes to the hub; no one sees
the tiers of seats begin to
circle sideways in the dark.

The play unfolds, the pace quickens,
the audience spins faster round its source
of action, its fantasy world.
The centrifugal pull strengthens,
tugging the spectator backwards,
(*as if a tiger flexed his paws*)
At this, heads turn uneasily,
'How did we get so far away?'
Latecomers fill the emptied rows;
'Can't we just stay to the end,
to see what happens, the meaning?'
Contemptuous, the force flings them out
to darkness, to the woods and stars:
(. . . *the tiger simply smiles* . . .)

The Bonfire

Throughout that summer the wisp of smoke
floated across the road in the woods.
Come September, it flared mad, scarlet,
frenzied with sparks in a needling wind.
October came the rains, and under cold
Orion the fire had surely died,
leaving just the warm brown pile it lived in.

Yet the next night it fingered its way
between trees, curling up to the stars.
Come the frosts of May, said the watchers,
it could well be smouldering still.

Parasols

On the terraces of hotels,
Or the decks of large cruise liners,
Or the patios of local pubs,
Rise up the ranks of parasols;
Closely tied for stormy weather,
arms high outstretched against the sun.

One hot night in the Midi,
when a storm began to brew,
when lightning flicked its fingers,
and the thunder rumbles grew,
the parasols threw off their ties,
out their panels swirled and flew,
backwards, forwards, frenziedly,
set to spin the whole night through.
A ballet corps of fury,
who believed that no one knew.

At sunrise, calm in lines they stood,
their laces tied, their skirts smoothed down,
as though the night had never been,
their secret wildness never seen;
they were mistaken. Someone saw.

Apples

He sat in the window, did the old man,
looking out over the gardens he loved,
kept his apples marching before him
on the sill, scarlet, russet and green.
He would lovingly recite their names
in the order they came to harvest,
Discovery, Elstar, Jonagold
Blenheim, Laxton, Lamborne, and Worcester
Round-eyed, his grandsons gazed at the row,
learning that sweetness needs time and sun,
and only comes from within the fruit.
They cupped hands round their chosen apple,
skipped to the door, and turned to wave goodbye.

Coast

Three cottages stood here by the shore,
before the sea swept in.
Their three owners sat in the gardens,
saw the tide inch nearer.

They watched its restless performances,
wind catspaws, crested waves,
ripples tiptoeing over the sands,
safe from the breaking surf.

Around this pageant the horizon
curved its arms, promising
as magnificent a world beyond
the cold shock of death.
So they waited and watched,
drawing comfort from uncertainty.

Hands

These hands which hold my driving keys
I turn palm upwards: my fingers show
bone and sinew, blood serving all.
In time the flesh will bleach to clay, and
scavengers throb under the soft skin.
Rook's call at twilight mocks a heart
raging, not at future darkness,
but that five great servants should die,
unacknowledged, and unrewarded.

My Arm Teedie

Bright and quick and silver haired,
Swift worker, fair and smiley,
Whom I loved, as children do,
As child I was allowed to see,
My Arn Teedie.

But never since I grew to now,
did she let me in again;
the safety distance, proper mask,
we both observed, me and
my Arn Teedie.

As though by living I became
suspect, traitor to the warmth
I wish we'd kept between our hands
to melt the ice in both our hearts,
my Arn Teedie

Moonset

Just as the moon withdraws her light from earth,
to walk a wider orbit not yet known,
So does my lover's light recede from me.

And as moonlight enfolds the sleeping hills,
lifting to beauty the already fair,
So does his love-light always lend me grace.

A billion years the moon will ride the clouds,
tugging tides, reflecting lovers' glory,
my lover's light must sink behind the hill.

Nouveau Venu
Joachim du Bellay (1522–1560)

Nouveau venu, qui cherches Rome en Rome,
Et rien de Rome en Rome n'apperçois,
Ces vieux palais, ces vieux arcs que tu vois,
Et ces vieux murs, c'est ce que Rome on nomme.

Vois quel orgueil, quelle ruine; et comme
Celle qui mit le monde sous les lois,
Pour dompter tout, se dompta quelquefois,
Et devint proie au temps, qui tout consomme

Rome de Rome est le seul monument,
Et Rome Rome a vaincu seulement.
Le Tybre seul, qui vers la mer s'enfuit,
Reste de Rome. O mondaine inconstance!
Ce qui est ferme, est par le temps détruit,
Et ce qui fuit, au temps fait résistance.

New Arrival

Newly arrived, who look for Rome in Rome,
And nothing of Rome, in Rome, can recognise,
These old walls, these towers before your eyes,
These palaces, are what is now called Rome.

Contemplate these ruins—and such conceit:
How she who gave the world its laws
Is now a prey to time, which all devours,
And conquering all, in turn endured defeat.

The only memorial of Rome is Rome,
Only Rome had power to conquer Rome;
Only the Tiber, which flows toward the sea,
Remains of Rome. O world of sand!
Where what stands firm, by time destroyed will be,
And what runs by, to time will make sure stand.

Ces Chères Mains
Paul-Marie Verlaine (1844–1896)

Les chères mains qui fûrent miennes,
Toutes petites, toutes belles,
Apres ces méprises mortelles
Et toutes ces choses paiennes,

Apres les rades et les grèves,
Et les pays et les provinces,
Royales mieux qu'au temps des princes
Les chères mains m'ouvrent les reves.

Mains en songe, mains sur mon âme,
Sais-je, moi, ce que vous daignâtes,
Parmi ces rumeurs scelerâtes,
Dire a cette âme qui se pâme?

Ment-elle, ma vision chaste,
D'affinité spirituelle,
De complicité natemelle,
D'affection étroite et vaste?

Remords si cher, peine très bonne,
Reves bénis, mains consacrees,
O ces mains, ses mains venerées,
Faites le geste qui pardonne!

Those Dear Hands

Those dear hands which once were mine,
so very small, so very rare;
through all the scorns I made you bear,
those savage acts whose guilt was mine,

Through all harbours, beyond all strands,
after countries, shires, all, have passed;
more royal than in kingly past,
dreams flower still from these dear hands.

Hands in dreams, these hands on my soul,
how can I know what you might say,
might stoop, through rumours foul display,
and still this fainting heart console?

Was it a lie, the long-held dream,
of a perfect soul's companion,
of a loving-close communion,
love in a huge yet channelled stream?

Remorse so dear, good pain, which lives
in blessed dreams, in hallowed hands,
O let these hands, these holy hands,
complete the gesture which forgives!

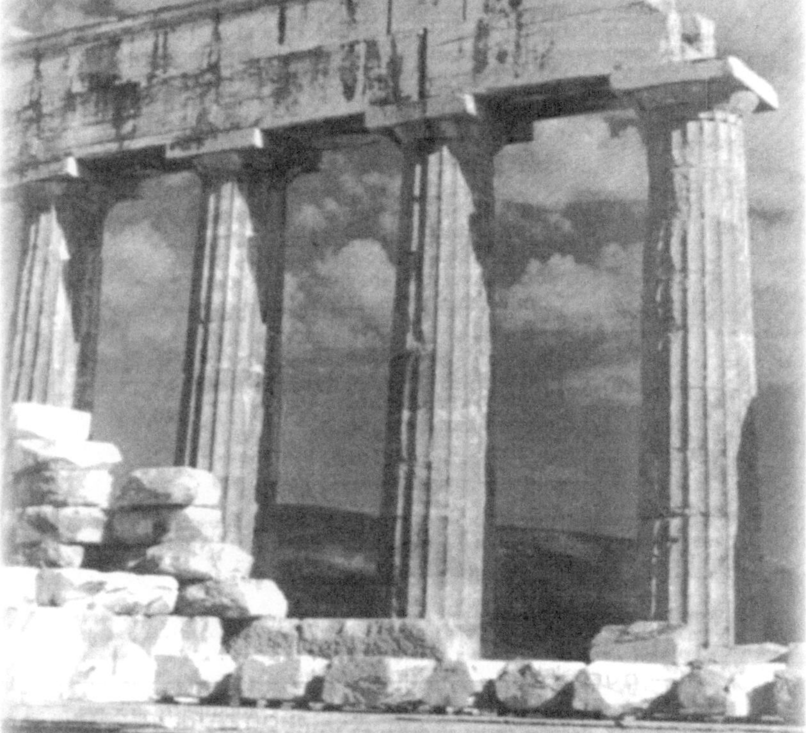

Cantique des Colonnes
(Paul Valéry 1871–1945)

Douces colonnes, aux
Chapeaux garnis de jour,
Ornés de vrais oiseaux
Qui marchent sur le tour,

Donées colonnes, ô
L'orchestre de fuseaux!
Chacun immole son
Silence a l'unisson.

—Que portez-vous si haut,
Égales radieuses?
—Au désir sans défaut
Nos grâces studieuses!

Nous chantons à la fois
Que nous portons les cieux!
O seule et sage voix
Qui chantes pour les yeux!

Vois quels hymnes candides!
Quelle sonorité
Nos éléments limpides
Tirent de la clarté!

Si froides et dorées
Nous fûmes de nos lits
Par le ciseau tirées,
Pour devenir ces lys!

De nos lits de cristal
Nous fûmes éveillées,
Des griffes de métal
Nous ont appareillées.

Pour affronter la lune.
La lune et le soleil,
On nous polit chacune
Comme ongle de l'orteil !

Servantes sans genoux,
Sourires sans figures,
La belle devant nous
Se sent les jambes pures.

Pieusement pareilles,
Le nez sous le bandeau
Et nos riches oreilles
Sourdes au blanc fardeau,

Un temple sur les yeux
Noirs pour l'éternité,
Nous allons sans les dieux
A la divinité !

Nos antiques jeunesses,
Chair mate et belles ombres,
Sont fières des finesses
Qui naissent par les nombres !

Filles des nombres d'or,
Fortes des lois du ciel,
Sur nous tombe et s'endort
Un dieu couleur de miel.

Il dort content, le Jour,
Que chaque jour offrons
Sur la table d'amour
Étale sur nos fronts.

Incorruptibles sœurs,
Mi-brûlantes, mi-fraîches,
Nous primes pour danseurs
Brises et feuilles sèches,

Et les siècles par dix,
Et les peuples passés,
C'est un profond jadis,
Jadis jamais assez!

Sous nos memes amours
Plus lourdes que le monde
Nous traversons les jours
Comme une pierre l'onde!

Nous marchons dans le temps
Et nos corps éclatants
Qnt des pas ineffables
Qui marquent dans les fables . . .

Song of the Columns

Smooth columns, hatted ready for morning,
carry live birds strolling on the crown.

Smooth columns, an orchestra of bobbins,
Each surrenders silence to unison.

'Radiant equals, what do you lift so high?'
'Our studied graces to flawless desire.

Singing together that we carry the skies,
deep single chord, heard only by the eyes

See our clear hymns, see the resonance
light itself gives to our lucid elements.

So golden; so cold: drawn by the chisel
out of our lode: shaped to these lilies.

We were awakened from our crystal bed,
With metal claws are we now embedded.

To confront the moon, the moon and the sun,
Like fingertip nails, polished each one.

Servants, not kneeling; smiles without faces
Beauty, on seeing us, knows true her bases

So meekly alike, and veiled by the frieze,
To its white burden, are deaf our carved ears.

Temple over the eyes, blind for all time;
without gods we rise—to the supreme being.

Ancient, our youth—matt flesh, sweet shadows—
Soars in subleties arising in number.

Golden seven's daughters, strong by heaven's laws,
on us falls, lazily sleeps, a honey-coloured god.

He sleeps well, does Day, serene on our bows,
whom we offer each day on the altar of love.

Sisters incorruptible, half cold, half warm,
Falling leaves, breeezes, caress us like dancers.

Centuries in tens, and races forgotten
fill a deepening past—never deep enough!

Lifting our own loves, heavier than the world,
we cleave through days as stone slices water.

We walk through time, and our brilliant bodies
leave mysterious prints, marching into legend . . .'

ACKNOWLEDGEMENTS

Thanks are due to the editors of the following publications in which some of my work has previously appeared: *Envoi*; *First Time*; and *Outposts*.

My work has also been awarded prizes in Norwich Writers' Circle competitions.